Water Shapes

An Ecocritical Anthology

Published through CreateSpace™ An Amazon Company

Printed in the United States of America
ISBN-13: 978-1979766791
ISBN-10: 1979766797

First Printing, 2017

Contents

Dedicated to those who helped me along
the road and became a place to rest. On
noons and midnights, thank you for being
my reprieve.

Introduction

To create an anthology is to weave a strong fabric using threads spun in works of differing times, places, motivations, and inspirations. Editors seek to find where authors use the same lens of language, form, and theme to draw out hidden features in vastly different work. Like a painter that swatches colors together to find complements and contrasts, not every work means the same thing on its own than when placed with others. I hope that I have achieved some kind of thematic harmony within this volume with the chosen quartet of works.

Ecology is often a field that brings to mind mosquito netting, public protests, bearded men, suntanned women, and lots of khaki pants. But the tradition of Ecological writing is a discipline that concerns us all, not divided from nature, but as part of it. We face a dangerous tide in our politics and our business that threatens to destroy the world we live in, piece by piece. The scripture of tame, domesticate, and consume is preached on every television, newspaper, and social media. The message is clear, use this world for material comfort and commodity. Who cares about the the Bonobo Monkeys that are dying out in the Congo? To that I say, well, we are apes too. It is not until we acknowledge our bodies, our human animal-ness, that we will ever be able to exist harmoniously with the natural world.

The pieces that I've collected here espouse the importance of our human animal. They talk of sacrifice, liberation, survival, and life. The threat to this world is human, but so is it's deliverance. They speak of choices, small human choices, and the nourishing presence of water, the lifeblood of the world. We must choose how we progress through the world.

If you have built castles in the air, your work need not be lost; that is where they should be. Now put the foundations under them.
-Henry David Thoreau

Growing the Green Place
The Gender Balanced Earth: Ecofeminism in *Mad Max: Fury Road*

Rose Watson

"My name is Max. My world is fire and blood" (Miller 0.00.20-0.00.24) these are the opening lines spoken in blackness while revving engines, the symphonic maelstrom of industrialization, echo in the background. And then we are welcomed into this terrifying world with a short history of the future. There is death: both violent and disease ridden. Water wars tear civilization apart. The damage we've done to the environment has finally leached into our own bodies creating humans born into what is known as half-life. Humanity is circling the drain, grasping at survival, not life. Carolyn Merchant speaks in Nature as Female, her essay on ecofeminism, that the earth is often historically and culturally tied to femaleness. Earth (and more broadly the environment) is seen as the great mother, life giver, and resource grower (10). She bears the wholeness of life and provides for it: the land her body, the water her blood, milk, and womb. In Max's world, nature has been raped, plundered, and disrespected, and now, she's angry. George Miller's film, *Mad Max: Fury Road* deftly connects the environment to the state of gender equality, showing his audience that when domination is the only way to sustain power, the whole world burns. The community formed throughout the film, spearheaded by Furiosa who embodies the duality of nature as both part of humanity and a force beyond it, discovers they need to create their own Eden by sacrifice and ideological change.

In Miller's new future, the world is less than a desert. The land is sour, desolate, and above all, dry. The land is a true wasteland, not in the definition that William Cronon uses in his essay, The Trouble with Wilderness; or, Getting Back to the Wrong Nature, in which he defines the modern concept of wilderness as a neutered, cultivated version of its older, pre-industrialization self. *Mad Max:*

Fury Road's wilderness is the old definition, the definition of men without metropolises to keep the wild world at bay. It is "savage, desolate, and barren [a place of] bewilderment –or terror" (Cronon 103). Feeding off the struggle of the natural world, other humans are more dangerous than any wild beast. Tribalism is the only form of protection, and to wander the wilderness alone is, well, mad. Merchant's vision of an ever-generous mother is replaced by a cracked husk, finally cutting the spoiled children off. Hang the consequences. This identity of hardened female power is echoed in the character of Furiosa, who becomes the analogue for a sustainable society that works with nature instead of against it. Furiosa is one of the strongest people in the film, but instead of using that power to dominate others, she uses it to free them. Much like nature is both a destructive and a nurturing force, Furiosa is a complex force to be reckoned with.

The earth's most valuable resource is missing from her landscape: water. There are no springs, wells, or rivers in this new world. Because of this great limiter, the tribes in this world find liquid wherever they can. The patriarchal head of Citadel, Immortan Joe, commodifies everything around him, including the source of his power, the life-giving fresh water that he pumps up from the depths of the earth, plundering her like the miners of old (Merchant 11). Joe controls his army of War Boys and a peasantry of wretched by manipulating the water source and using nature as a tool. He selectively lets it pour down to the people below, enough to allow them to survive, but not enough to ever quench their thirst saying, "Do not, my friends, become addicted to the water. It will take hold of you, and you will resent its absence" (Miller 0.09.00-0.10.00). In this way, he also demonizes the natural water as something addictive and dangerous. Only he is strong enough to protect them from this dangerous element. The warlord further commodifies the water, branding it Aqua-Cola, and barters it with two other strongholds (Miller 01.27.15). He sends his War Boys (all half-life humans) out on scavenging trips to attack and capture any small tribes or wanderers. Full-

10

blooded humans are then caged and used as living blood bags to pro-
long dying War Boys, showing another way that Joe's cult consumes
the world around them. This also demonstrates the futility of Joe's
system as he fuels healthy resources into poisoned ones instead of
attempting to cure the root illness. Humans, after all, are part of the
natural environment and are thus treated with the same consumption
as Joe treats the water. The titular character, Max, is brought to Citadel as a particularly valuable blood bag: a universal donor. Water and
blood are resources in the highest regard in this world. They provide
life, but are also used to control. Because Immortan Joe supplies
both, there is no escape from relying on him and becoming ensnared
in his system of manipulation.

Water is continually used as a focal metaphor for rebirth, pu-
rity, and growth. Max suffers from PTSD-like flashbacks that throw
him back to sounds and images of the people he failed to protect,
especially his young daughter. These flashbacks are strongest when
there is water around such as the opening scenes of Max attempting
escape from Citadel and when he confronts the wives for the first
time after the sandstorm (Miller 00.04.38, 00.32.50). The cleans-
ing of the water is harsh; it forces Max to confront what he lost and
remember his identity. In the opening monologue Max states, "I
exist in this wasteland… a man reduced to a single instinct: survive"
telling us that when he is pitted against the wasteland his identity is
forfeit (Miller 00.03.06). It is only as Max allows himself to accept his
human identity back with the aid of Furiosa and the wives that he
can begin to heal. Max is a "raging feral" in Citadel while he's locked
in a cage being used as a blood bag, his own life-water being stolen
from him (Miller 00.16.08). But when he is freed from his IV and
muzzle by the trust of Furiosa, he begins to heal. That healing is only
improved over the course of the movie as he bonds with the women,
Nux (a reformed War Boy), and the Vuvalini. The bonded group of
Max, Furiosa, Nux, and the wives is the healthiest community we see
in the film, and the only one capable of creating The Green Place, the

Eden of this world.

We see two communities throughout the film, both of which are unsustainable and dying. Immortan Joe's Citadel is deeply patriarchal. Internally, he links his power to his lineage and phallus. He calls his War Boys his sons. He creates an image of himself as great father, protector, and punisher who will usher them into death and then new life in the next world. He becomes the God of Life and Death. He wears the symbol of his Citadel over his crotch, the very same symbol that is branded on every War Boy, captured slave, and servant in his territory, making them symbolic products of his virility. The Immortan's symbol is even carved into the face of the rock towers that make up the stronghold, claiming the environment as under his dominion. Even his vehicle, the Gigahorse, is two chassis mounted one atop the other in a bestial mating formation. His war attire features a violent codpiece that frames his crotch with two pistols, symbolizing that he has power over life and death.

Immortan Joe keeps a harem of full-life, healthy, and beautiful wives (The Splendid Angharad, Capable, The Dag, Cheedo, and Toast) for the express purpose of birthing a viable heir to his domaine. Despite the effort Joe has put into creating an identity of complete control over the natural world, his own natural weakness betrays him. He seeks to place himself above the natural world, but cannot escape that he is man, and therefore part of it. He has two sons already, but they are both disabled. They are symptoms of the unhealthy bloodline of an old, rotting man trying to create something eternal. His wives are, "breeders. His prize breeders" and, in his eyes, another resource to be owned, consumed, and destroyed (Miller 0.15.19). These five women are the real key to Immortan Joe's immortality.

Joe's War Boy cult is made up exclusively of boys and young men. These men have no connection to the natural world around hem to the extent that even their bodies are foreign. Their environment is spoken of in mechanical terms. Nux calls the wives "shiney" and "so chrome" instead of beautiful or healthy, relating them to the most coveted of machinery: that which isn't rusted. The doctor of the Citadel is named Organic Mechanic, showing their full ignorance of even their own flesh and blood bodies. War Boys cover themselves in scarifications of mechanical assemblages (V8 engines, hydraulic pumps, and shocks) converting their natural flesh into something unnatural, but which they understand better. Gasoline is known as "guzzoline" a term that connects it with the act of consuming. One of the nearby towns that Citadel trades with is even called Bullet Farm. Between this reassignment of natural identity, Joe's commodification and manipulation of natural resources, and the War Boys' ignorance, the bond between society and nature is all but completely severed in Citadel. By denying that they are part of nature as human beings, the citizens of Citadel become destructive to their environment and themselves. They have resources, but no connection to the environment to benefit that connection.

The other community on the brink of extinction is the Vuvalini, or better known as the Many Mothers. The little we know about them is from Furiosa's childhood memory and the few women we meet in the third act of the film. The Many Mothers are, as the name suggests, a matriarchy and, though they are not as domineering and cruel as Citadel, are still dying out. The Vuvalini that are left are post-menopausal women, with no men in their group at all. Unlike Joe's cult, the Vuvalini are uniquely, positively connected to the earth. They travel nomadically on motorcycles using only what they can carry. They have knowledge of the old world, and the medical terms for the body. They even have a collection of seeds, all which is left of their home, to plant in a new place when the opportunity arises. They are guardians of nature. But every seed The Keeper of the Seeds plants dies due to sour earth and too little water (Miller 01.23.40). They have the connection, but not the resources to thrive with nature. While the Vuvalini are presented in a positive light with intelligence, wisdom, and a respect for the world around them, they are still dying. In this way, the film indicates that the Vuvalini are unfit to bring back the Green Place. But there is one person who is.

Furiosa is the bridge between worlds. She was born Vuvalini but grew up War Boy. She is both a paternal protector and maternal support. Splendid and The Dag may both be pregnant, but Furiosa is the true mother of the revolution. But more than that, Furiosa is an embodiment of feminist nature. Merchant references early Christian thought about gender balance saying, "nature… consisted of a unity of equally male-female principals" (17). Furiosa embodies this balance, showing how uniting the male and female societies of the film creates strength and sustainability. She's not just running from the Citadel's patriarchal control; she's going to her home that relies on two things: thriving nature and feminine dignity. It is in the name: The Green Place of Many Mothers. Furiosa survives the film, regardless of being put in peril more than almost any other character, echoing how nature still persists. Furiosa does not see herself as human apart from nature, but human as part of nature. Furiosa's first escape is through a raging sandstorm. She runs to the most wild and deadly form of nature available to her, and, almost as if it sees her kinship with it, she and her wards are protected. Her vehicle is the only one that survives the storm, those who chase her are thrown into tornadoes and engulfed by lighting (Miller 00.28.22). We see the same wrath and terror in Furiosa when she fights. She rages in the same intensity. And when she fights she fights for survival and protection, unlike the War Boys who tussle and fight to establish dominance and rank. Furiosa is like a mother bear: powerful, but not reckless. Furiosa is fully part of the world around her, as well as a synthesis of cultures.

The characters who survive the final battle demonstrate the needs of the Green Place they seek to establish. The wives are liberated individuals searching for human dignity. Max is an individual wanderer looking for identity. One of the Vuvalini survives to pass on history and knowledge. Furiosa is the embodiment of nature. These features will try to fix the toxic features of their current system, but they can only do so if they work together. There is no moment that shows this importance more than the drive back to the Citadel after the final battle. Furiosa is dying after killing Immortan Joe. She is exsanguinated from a wound on her side, much like the world around her. She has no blood; the environment has no water. But the group sacrifices to save her. Nux sacrifices his life, destroying the toxic system he embodied to save the group from being overrun. The one Vuvalini left gives her knowledge of medicine to diagnose her injuries. The wives comfort Furiosa the way she always comforted them. And Max, this time voluntarily, gives his blood, using the very same IV that was draining his life in the first act of the film. It is this joint sacrifice that will save nature and rebuild the Green Place over the ruins of the Citadel. This scene of sacrifice to Furiosa demonstrates the sacrifices that society must make to work with the natural world, instead of consuming it. It shows the shift in perspective from a need to dominate to a desire to cooperate.

The wretched welcome Furiosa and the war rig home. When they call for the group to be lifted into the Citadel, a place they've never been allowed to go, the wives pull the wretched up with them (Miller 01.51.02). As Furiosa rises into safety, water is freed to fall down to those who so desperately need it. Nature is set free and brought to a position of respect. As the film closes, it leaves us with hope for this new society where War Boys work with wretched and women, to create a better place, a place full of green.

References

Cronon, William. "The Trouble with Wilderness; Or, Getting Back to the Wrong Nature Ecocriticism: The Essential Reader", Edited by Ken Hiltner, Routledge, 2015, pp. 102–119.

Gaard, G. "New Directions for Ecofeminism: Toward a More Feminist Ecocriticism." Interdisciplinary Studies in Literature and Environment, vol. 17, no. 4, Jan. 2010, pp. 643–665. EBSCO Host, doi:10.1093/isle/isq108.

Miller, George, director. Mad Max: Fury Road . Warner Bros. Pictures , 2015.

Merchant, Carolyn. "Nature as Female ." Ecocriticism: The Essential Reader", Edited by Ken Hiltner, Routledge, 2015, pp. 10–34.

The Single Greatest Achievement of All Mankind

Jared De Roo

Earth had not been visible for some time now, to the lone spacecraft. It sat as a single dot in a velvet universe. Though it moved quickly, its progress was invisible against the vastness of space laid out around it. A little blue plume of fire from the thrusters was the only real indication that it was moving at all. Sputtering along for months before it would be able to begin any real progress.

In the tiny ship there lived five even smaller humans. Each of them, in their own way, remembered how big everything had felt back on Earth. The ship, a colossus, towering above any monument of human achievement. Themselves giants among mankind, chosen for glorious purpose. They all felt very small now. Even the blanket of stars seemed to have faded away, leaving only the jet blackness.

It was a couple weeks into the voyage when space began to close in on them. As the stars receded and the ship became enveloped in darkness, the vastness of space seemed to condense into the little microcosm of the ship, and nothing else.

Behind the treated glass panes of the little vessel, two faces stared absently out into the void. One a dark haired woman with a mousy face, the other a light haired man with a square jaw. They both stared, silently, out into the blackness. There had been a lot of talking during the first couple months of the journey. During the third month, when the tightness of space had really begun to set in it had sort of tapered off. Everyone had sort of receded into themselves, they all knew what to do. Routine dominated their lives, there really ust wasn't much to say anymore.

The woman stared at the console in front of her. Silently wishing for the day, if you could call it that, to end. She was ready for the routine to be shaken up a little, tomorrow the mission would really begin.

"Are you scared, Ali?"

She started, annoyed that Hans had broken the unspoken rule of silence, "I just want something to happen." She paused, unsure of whether or not she actually wanted to continue the conversation, "Are you?"

"Yah, a little."

"It should be safe."

Hans didn't respond, instead he turned back, let his eyes glaze over, and continued staring out into space.

━ Four Hours Before Mankind's First Jump to Light Speed ━

Jack was nervous and everyone knew it. He'd had a small mental break a few weeks ago, they'd forced him to take on extra video sessions with the mission psychologist. He was doing okay now. He mostly stayed in the lab with Hoshi, there wasn't much to do it this point. They'd check and recheck the equipment, go over the lists of samples they'd need, inspect crew biometrics, stare at the wall, and do it all again.

Over the last few days most of what they'd accomplished was making sure that they'd gotten the last of the crumbs from some sort of food Ali had brought into the lab. The lab needed to be sterile. Without gravity the little bits had floated off into seemingly every corner of the room. They'd just finished vacuuming the room for the third time, just hoping that it wouldn't wind up contaminating anything. Though Jack did think it'd be funny if they came back with amples showing signs of nutrigrain bars from other planets.

"Are we ready for tomorrow?" A thick Russian voice barked a the door to the lab opened.

"We are ready, Anna." Hoshi said absently.

Jack nodded along vigorously, "Yup, we've got everything. Just really waiting on positioning and that, you know. Ship should be where we need it in-" he paused and looked over at a timer built into the wall, "four hours. Then uh, then we can make the jump."

"Good." Anna looked around the room once more before closing the door.

As the sound of her magnetic boots faded down the hall, Jack turned to Hoshi, "She still scares me."

Hoshi was silent for a second, "She is unpleasant."

"Yeah, something like that. I just don't know what it is but something is weird about her."

"Maybe, but you would do better to worry more about the jump and less about Anna."

— Six Minutes Before Mankind's First Jump to Light Speed —

The whole crew sat huddled in front of the control panel in the cockpit of the ship. The wave of melancholy that had filled the ship for the last few months had lifted, leaving a nervous tension. Anna's fingers tapped the console in an arrhythmic beat, her grey eyes staring intently at the timer embedded in the console.

"Do you think we'll find it?"

Anna started. Everyone was silent.

"You know, find life?" Hans continued, nervous but excited.

Still no one responded. Anna had still not gotten used to Hans' nervous chatter that had plagued the crew since departure.

Hans didn't continue. Instead he too turned to the console. Five more minutes.

Jack's breathing got heavier as the countdown continued, Hoshi noted. His lack of nerves had been grating on her, but in this moment even she was beginning to feel the knot in her stomach tighten as the countdown continued. Four more minutes.

Anna's fingers tapped faster, her eyes fixated on the timer. Three more minutes.

Jack wasn't feeling great. The old feeling of panic flared up. He was paralyzed where he stood, praying it would pass when they made the jump. Two more minutes.

Ali was ready to vomit. One more minute.

━Mankind's First Jump to Light Speed ━

The zeros expanded into infinity as the countdown completed, splitting reality down the middle. There was a weird moment in the nanosecond between the end of the timer and the start of the jump that lasted forever. Each moment zeroed into a tight focus and exploding beyond cognition as the universe condensed itself into the now and spread that brief frame of being into eternity. The crew themselves felt suddenly infinite.

Their souls squeezed from their bodies as their conscious expanded across the universe, looking deeply into every moment at once only to bounce back and forth from every point in time and space melding together into a single bodiless mass.

And then it ended.

The weird blur of eternity closed and each crew member was left, pale faced, in their own body, feeling so small.

The silence that followed seemed endless. Everyone still in shock from the moment. The complete separation from physicality as if their bodies had moved too quickly for their souls to follow and they were just now catching up.

Jack collapsed.

Everyone, for a moment, was frozen in space, Jack hit the ground with a muted thud. Each member of the crew stood like statues until the moment caught up with them. In a second the stillness was broke. The ship shuddered as life resumed. As if someone had slammed the brakes on a fast moving car. The stillness shattered into explosive motion as the crew was thrown forward onto the console. Jack's crumpled body slammed into the glass viewport before beginning to drift listlessly around the cabin.

Anna was the first to resume motion. Her eyes darted to Jack. The others were slowly picking themselves off the floor as she disabled the magnetism in her boots and floated up to Jack. His breathing was shallow, but he seemed to be alive. She noted that one of his feet, bootless, was bent at a weird angle. Broken when the boot hadn't left the cabin floor at the same speed he did.

"Hans, help me with Jack." She ordered down.

Hans helped the two of them back to the cabin floor, with Anna back on the ground the two of them secured Jack to one of the seats.

"He's breathing. We need to do something about his foot." Anna said as she buckled Jack to the chair.

"I'll grab the med kit." Ali said quickly as she rushed out of the cabin, shaken.

"Well," Hans began, "Did we make it?" He stared out of the cabin window, the blackness had erupted into a star studded universe.

Hoshi surveyed the panel, "We made it. Everything worked. Everything but..." She paused and looked more closely.

"Everything but what?" Anna asked.

"I don't know, but look here," She motioned to the two of them, "At the very beginning of the jump, there's nothing there."

Anna pushed her aside to look for herself. There was indeed a small break in the trajectory, as if the ship had simply vanished for a second.   "Probably just an error." She said.

"Probably just an error." Jack repeated.

The three of them snapped their heads around to follow the voice. Jack was sitting up, slowly beginning to unbuckle himself.

"Stay in the chair, Jack." Anna ordered, "You broke your ankle." She stared down at him, wondering if maybe he was in shock.

"Broke my ankle." Jack repeated, following Anna's inflection.

"You're in shock, Jack. Just stay still." Hans stepped towards him.

Anna almost reached out to stop him, but caught herself.

◾Ten Minutes After Mankind's First Jump to Light Speed ◾

Ali stood still in the supply closet for a few minutes. Just breathing. Something wasn't right and she knew it. She took a deep breath. She was here for the med kit. Just grab the med kit, she told herself. She had seen something during the jump. A brief moment, a split second. Somewhere between the jump and infinity, that second of forever before they hit light speed something had slipped onto the ship. She remembered that as her soul flowed out her eyes in the brief in-between there was a wisp of black tendrils snaking across the exterior of the ship. She could've sworn she saw it swirling inside of Jack before she returned to her own body. The med kit.

"Ali." Anna's voice cracked through her earpiece, "Return to the bridge. We do not need the med kid. Return to the bridge. We're going home."

Ali froze. Anna may not have been the most polished person, but her voice seemed to have the quality of someone just learning to speak a new language.

"Ali, we're going home."

She tapped the button on her transmitter, "I-I'm on my way back." A wave of dread washed over her as she made her return to the bridge.

◾Twenty Five Minutes After Mankind's First Jump to Light Speed◾

"Are we authorized to return without samples?" Ali asked nerously.

"We are authorized to return without samples." Hans stared directly at her, a sickly sort of smile fixed on his lips.

This wasn't right. None of this was right. Ali tried to suppress her panic. She had checked through the instrument board to find nothing, except a minor blip in the readings, out of place. There was no reason to head back, not that she could think of at least. "Um, Anna, w-why are we going back? The ship's reading everything fine."

"Orders." Anna smiled.

"We…we can't receive transmissions after the jump, Anna." Ali moved to stand out of her seat. Before she could get to her feet she felt a hand on her shoulder. Hans weighed down on her, softly but firmly.

"We need to get Jack home, Ali." Hans motioned somberly towards Jack.

"We need to get me home, Ali." Jack stepped forward, his ankle making a hideous crack under his shifting weight.

"Hans…Jack…"Ali's apprehension turned to dread, "We have orders, we need to collect the samples."

Anna moved closer, "There is not time. We need to get home soon."

"But Anna, the ship's fine, Jack…Jack will be fine…we have provisions. We're prepared for things like this." Ali's voice cracked as the tone of the room darkened.

"That's an order, Ali." Anna's voice sharpened.

"Okay." Ali sat silently for a second. Something in the pit of her stomach was beginning to clench. "Hans?"

Hans stared, unmoving.

"Hans, I need your help to reset the jump drive. I can't do this alone."

Hans hesitated, "Are you certain?"

Ali was taken aback, "What do you mean? You have the other key, I can't access the controls without it. We just did this."

Anna stepped up, "Take his key, you need to do this without him."

"I don't understand is something wrong?" Ali's heart sank.

"Ali, please just take us home." Hoshi's voice cracked.

"I…"Ali began to choke up, she took a pause, swallowed, and shakily continued, "I don't know what's happening right now."

Jack lurched forward, "Ali, are you okay?" His ankle was beginning to soak in red.

Hans spent an awkward moment searching himself for the key, he found it hung around his neck. "Here's my key."

"Just…Just put it in the keyhole there," She pointed to the other side of the panel, "We'll turn them at the same time…like before."

Hans fumbled with his key, it took them a couple tries to sync up their key turns, even though they'd done this hundreds of times in training. Ali felt a bead of sweat forming on her forehead. "Why are we going home, Anna?"

Anna stared at her for a moment, "We're running low on food."

"We just took stock before the jump though, we have enough for at least another year."

Anna's face tightened. "I am running low on food." She stared pointedly at Ali. "Take us home. Now."

Ali froze. Four pairs of eyes glared down at her. For a moment no one spoke, Ali began to feel as if the world was growing around her and she was, all of a sudden, very small.

"Now." Anna growled, placing a threatening hand on her shoulder.

Ali hesitated at the controls for a moment, contemplating the consequences of what she was about to do. Finally, with half a strangled sob, she gritted her teeth, and began setting up the sequence. "I need your fingerprint, Anna." She whispered as she shakily completed the operation.

Anna smiled, removed her hand from Ali's shoulder, and authenticated the launch sequence. Ali felt her heart sink as the autopilot locked.

The world didn't bend around them this time. Rather it skipped in a sickening lurch as the ship began to jettison fuel reserves, blasting forward at full power with what was left in the tanks. A muted sob escaped Ali.

"Ali, why is the ship not jumping." Anna's voice carried a tinge of panic.

Ali stayed silent.

Anna leapt forward, lifted her from her seat, and in a single motion threw her against console. "What did you do?" She barked.

Ali's eyes flinched to the quickly emptying fuel gauge.

Hoshi jumped to the controls, but paused before touching them, hands prepared but frozen, as if trying to remember how they worked. "Fix it, Ali!" She finally screamed.

Ali set her jaw, "I can't."

Four pairs of eyes locked on her. "Take us home, Ali." They said in unison.

Ali closed her eyes, "I won't." She whispered.

■Two Thousand Years After Mankind's First Jump to Light Speed ■

The little ship, almost invisible against the black felt canvas behind it, hurdled along through the universe. Momentum fueling its eternal voyage. The rockets had died out long ago. Now the speck was free to sail along the infinite expanse without interruption. Millions of miles past and trillions of miles to go. The ship was in no hurry and the universe would be there a while yet, so the little craft sailed on.

The Sound of A Wild Ecocriticist Eating

Kayla Peifer

In *The Sound of a Wild Snail Eating*, Elisabeth Bailey poetically describes her life after becoming bedridden with an illness affecting her nervous system. Through her days of low activity, she is brought together with a wild snail that, eventually, helps Bailey mentally take a step away from her sickness to notice the environment around her. Even as someone who was a profound naturalist, moving this close to cohabitation and intimacy with nature was a shift for Bailey. The coexistence between humans and nature has changed over time from a mutual relationship, to one species establishing a hierarchy over the other. In other words, humans have gone from living with nature to having a sense of dominion over it.

Bailey's theme throughout the writing is the restoration of the connection between nature and humans. One of the best examples of this is the connection between the snail and Bailey. The snail becomes an agent for Bailey to reflect on life through. Bailey also used the presence of the snail to move through her own journey with illness. It is evident that Bailey connected both her story and her personality with the simplicity and slow movement of the snail. Bailey also introduces important moments in her story such as: the presence of the snail, the relationship between Bailey and the snail, Bailey's illness in relation to the snail, and the idea of taking time to look at the nature around us.

Paul Shepard's writing on ecology and human influence analyzes a viewpoint also found throughout Bailey's work of fiction. Shepard writes that ecology faces the task of "renewing a balanced view where now there is human-centeredness, even pathology of isolation and fear" (Shepard 62). Bailey addresses this in her creative piece in a way that is subtle, yet omnipresent in the text. At one oint, Bailey describes a point where her nurse is helping her gather dirt and plants for her snail's terrarium. At first, the terrarium is filled with dirt and foliage from around where they are staying. After thought and research, Bailey has her nurse help her gather pieces of nature that would be from the snail's natural environment, thus creating a better ecosystem for the snail to live in. Shepard relates to this by saying that the relationship between humans and ecology is one that needs to focus on finding a balance between nature and human. Shepard continues by saying that the image of human influence on nature is stylized to "fit the fixed curves of our vision" (63). Shepard argues that if humans were to work on finding an ideal relationship between humans and nature, we would in turn naturally work towards fixing the current relationship. Shepard brings up the point as well that humans are in this "web of life" manipulating the strands rather than simply living. Both Bailey and Shepard focus on the idea that our view today is that while we may be physically surrounded by nature, we often forget that we are living side by side with other species. We share the natural environment. Like the original nurse who filled the terrarium with whatever was easiest to find, humans manipulate the world around us in the convenient ways rather than what would be ideal for both nature and humans.

Other theorists note the current separation between humans and nature. Lynn White Jr. wrote, "formerly man had been part of nature; now he was the exploiter of nature" (42). Throughout the story of her time with the snail, Bailey is taken aback by what she discovers about the world around her. Bailey notes in her book, "The life of a snail is as full of tasty food, comfortable beds of sorts, and a mix of pleasant and not-so-pleasant adventures as that of anyone I know" (Bailey 98). This is the type of relationship that we should have with nature. Bailey studies the movements, eating habits, and patterns of the snail in order to keep from focusing on her own illness. Bailey even states at one point in the creative writing that she begins to worry about how far the snail will travel at night, the difficulties it may encounter, and what risky item it may choose as a meal (26). The overall idea and hope is to not only survive, but to live together and nurture one another. Bailey clearly relates to the snail in human terms, as if she is worrying about a close friend or family member. Bailey's mindset is an important perspective for mankind to focus on. As a race that lives off of natural ecosystems, it is important that we take time to both worry and protect that environment that sustains our everyday life. While the text isn't saying every citizen needs to become an environmental specialist, it is important for everyone to know that importance and impact that nature has on human existence.

If our species continues its current relationship with nature, it is clear that we will have an everlasting dominion over nature rather than a coexisting peaceful connection. While we may never be powerless to the natural world, there is still a need to exercise control in how we use our power and discover better ways to control the environment around us. Bruno Latour touches on this idea in his writing, "What Is To Be Done? Political Ecology!" Latour focuses on a human's power within our own society and our need to exercise individual power. "No one is asking you to abandon all power, but simply to exercise it as a power, with all its precautions, its slowness, its procedures, and especially its checks and balances" (Latour 233). This concept Latour presents relates to the human's overwhelming desire for dominion over other things. For Bailey, this included using her power to correct the habitat that the snail was living in, changing the easy and quick approach for one that was more time consuming, yet beneficial long term. Latour continues by saying that by losing nature, our public life also loses our principal cause of our "paralysis" (Latour 234). By removing what we consider a threat to our "natural" human-made life, we lose the environment that we need in order to survive.

One of the final points from Bailey's writing is how important it is that we take a step back from our lives to, even passively, observe the nature around us. For Bailey, this was observing and studying the snail to take her mind off of the illness that seemed to overwhelm her life. When studying the snail, Bailey found what she considered the best sentence to describe a snail's way of life: "The right thing to do is to do nothing, the place to do it is in a place of concealment, and the time to do it is as often as possible" (Bailey 116). In "The Trouble with Wilderness; Or, Getting Back to the Wrong Nature," William Cronan writes that the time has come to rethink what we consider wilderness (Cronan 102). Cronan continues by saying that wilderness is the place where we try to "withhold our power to dominate" (Cronan 115). Hundreds of years ago, what we knew as "wilderness" was something that was considered "deserted" and "savage," where as today it is something that we strive to take control of. We may not find the wilderness as "savage" as we once did, but our need for dominion over it needs to change into more of an observational view.

Cronan continues by saying that "learning to honor the wild—learning to remember and acknowledge the autonomy of the other—means striving for critical self-consciousness in all of our actions" (Cronan 117). In turn, one of Bailey's points was that she dreamt of a time where humans could follow in the "footsteps" of snails by hibernating during times of trouble. She writes that if humans with illnesses could "simply go dormant while the scientific world went about its snail-paced research" (Bailey 109). Both of these statements by Cronan and Bailey focus on the idea that we could greatly benefit even by simple observation and mimicking the simplicity of the nature around us.

While Bailey's writing focuses on her mental and physical journey with the help of a wild snail, the writing shows a deeper connection to those willing to find it. From the writing, Bailey explains that there is a significant impact on life when one takes time to step away and observe the world around them. She finds herself focusing more on the snail's adventures and lifestyle rather her personal troubles. Lynn White Jr. writes, "What people do about their ecology depends on what they think about themselves in relation to things around them" (White 43). Bailey has learned to live and react differently because of her relationship and interaction with the snail.

In her work, Bailey brings the connection between human beings and nature to a realistic everyday view. She brings her personal life into nature and tells the captivating connect she personally made with nature. If we as not only a society but also a species could expand this connection to each of our lives, the two ecosystems of humans and nature would be able to live a closer life as one rather than two separate habitats hoping to survive one another.

References

Bailey, Elisabeth Tova. The Sound of A Wild Snail Eating. Algonquin Books of Chapel Hill, 2010.

Cronan, William. The Trouble With Wilderness; Or, Getting Back To The Wrong Nature. Ecocriticism: The Essential Reader, edited by Ken Hiltner, Routledge, 2015, pp. 102-117.

Latour, Bruno. What Is To Be Done? Political Ecology! Ecocriticism: The Essential Reader, edited by Ken Hiltner, Routledge, 2015, pp. 232-236.

Shepard, Paul. Ecology and Man: A Viewpoint. Ecocriticism: The Essential Reader, edited by Ken Hiltner, Routledge, 2015, pp. 62-69.

White, Lynn Jr. The Historical Roots of Our Ecological Crisis. Ecocriticism: The Essential Reader, edited by Ken Hiltner, Routledge, 2015, pp. 39-46.

When the Girl Fell

Rose Watson

"Nature's creative power is far beyond man's instinct of destruction."
—Jules Verne

The girl didn't know when the wing hit her. One moment she was darting across a bridge, the familiar thrum of the metal support ropes echoing in her shins, and the next… She was flying. For half a second she hung, frozen and suspended in the air, a true flying fish. And then the ringing in her head came into focus. A warm feeling coated her temple and then her cheek and the wind began to push at her clothes and limbs. She had a moment to turn toward the sea, sparkling below.

She plummeted.

~~~~~~~~

"Do you taste it, sister?" the raw edge of the old man's voice had broken the calm of the early morning meditation. An uncomfortable murmur rumbled through the congregation. The captain had been silent for thirteen months. He had been in the middle of a sermon when the tide drew out. They said that the sea took his voice because she loved the way it sounded. No one knew if she'd ever give it back.

"Do you taste it?" he said again, looking to the woman sitting to his right. The congregation had gotten used to going through the meditations and services with a mute leader, and no one had taken on more service than Lorelei, a tired twenty something who had found purpose in the small, fervent community of the Church of Our
~~~~~~~~

Tidal Mother. She was staring, eyes wide, at her captain.

"I don't…"

"Do you taste it girl! The air is flowing with salt this day. A great wave is coming for our city. We will see the way that the mother protects her children." The old man, stood suddenly and strode through the circle of faithful. They parted in stunned silence, hanging on the words of the old man. He hadn't moved this easily since before the rot. The staff he had relied on for the past four years was abandoned at his seat, "Yes my friends! Can you taste it? This is the dawn of a blessed day. We must welcome it!"

He had reached the solid double doors of the chapel. They were big and sturdy, made of the recycled side paneling of a retired naval ship. The captain grabbed the handles of the doors and pulled, dragging them open in one motion. He stood, his full body haloed with light from the sun breeching over the horizon of the sea. Lorelei had stumbled after him, desperate to help her guru, but stopped at seeing his eyes streaming with tears. They flowed down his face, and he made no move to wipe them away.

"Sister," his voice had hushed so only Lorelei could hear him, "I am called. I leave my ship to you." The old man died.

<center>~~~~~~~</center>

The girl had been born decades after the city drowned. She'd heard stories of the dry city, how there was pavement and sidewalks and most people owned dogs or cats. She had seen old photos of dry boats that used to fill the streets from morning to night; Miss Angela, the old lady who she paged to quite often, had called them cars. Miss Angela told her once that you couldn't even see the ocean from the street when she was a girl. The levees were too high. She and her friends would go on picnics on the crown of the levee and joke about how the world would end. Miss Angela would get very quiet after saying things like this. The girl found it odd, because the world hadn't ended after all. But she didn't tell Miss Angela that.

Five million people died after the first flooding. Another four and a half died after the second rupture. But the real killer was the skin rot. Something in the sea reacted to the sealant on the streets and a toxic element was formed. It leeched into the bodies of refugees. It saturated the relief food and the blankets that were constantly damp and musty. Curing it was easy: stay dry. But that wasn't as simple as it sounded. Eventually, Neheti Crane developed a sort of cure, and like a crusading hero, proclaimed the safety of the people bellow while selling each injection at a price. Ten million more people rotted away while the city began to rebuild.

Cults began to crop up begging forgiveness and protection from the sea. Some begged help from the Virgin Mary, others Poseidon, merfolk, Lí Ban, Lir, Mazu, Samundra, Yemoja, and countless others. New prophets claimed to be able to heal the skin rot. Some just wanted to create new families when all others were lost. The girl's parents didn't believe in much of anything anymore. They used to, but there is only so much you can hold onto. The girl just liked the songs that she could hear from the small chapels built on the lower deck where she lived.

～～～～～

"You absolute imbecile!" Dr. Reiksac been waiting for him to land on the wide balcony that jutted out from the side of the laboratory floor. He could see through the broad windows of the lab that all her assistants and researchers were gone.

"This was not my fault." The man stripped off his gloves and threw them on the ground.

"Like hell this wasn't your fault! What kind of egotist flies unfinished tech in between decks?"

"I had control," his voice came out clearer as he took off the helmet, "You told me to put the wing-suit through its paces; I did. You were the one that designed the safety protocols to freeze out the goddamn pilot!"

"You should never have flown in between bridges and promenades. The programming had an error; that's what this experiment was for! Finding problems. Not endangering civilians before we're even on the market!" In anger, Dr. Reiksac threw a clipboard to the ground, splaying papers across the sleek, black floor of the lab.

"I wouldn't have if your tech had worked right!" There were a few moments of silence. Barron Holiday could see Dr. Reiksac was seething as she glared at him. Her fists had gone as white as her lab coat from being clenched. He was sweating and breathing hard. He broke the staring contest to stumble to a carafe of cold water. Holiday poured himself a shaky glass and downed it, falling into a chair by the counter.

"Did you see what happened to her?" Dr. Reiksac's voice had lost its hot fury and had gone ice cold.

"She fell."

"No shit, Holiday." the pilot wiped a hand down his face.

"She popped out of nowhere. The proximity alarm went off; it froze me out. I couldn't pull up or retract the wings. I tried to roll, but I didn't have time." Dr. Reiksac took a deep breath and pushed her shiny black hair back from her face. She stepped to the counter and rested her knuckles on the cool surface.

"She was young too. We are going to be crucified for this one. At least she wasn't anyone's daughter." Holiday stared at her as she pushed off the counter and pulled up a command screen, deftly opening several message windows to send to various assistants and PR personnel.

"What do you mean she wasn't anyone's daughter, of course she was!" he poured himself another glass. Dr. Reiksac didn't turn around.

"Yes, but not to anyone important."

〜〜〜〜〜

The girl got the page job when she turned ten. She had lived most of her life dashing around the lower decks and, like any child born in the drowned city, had natural sea legs. She could run across a choppy intersection with an open jug of water without spilling a drop. She'd taken the lid off of one just to see if she could. While paging didn't pay well, it was something to contribute to their families. The girl's mother, Tala, spent a week's wages on good sturdy boots for her and dubbed the girl her, "little flying fish". Most people in the lower decks would call after her as she darted up the creaking staircases and whipped around corners.

〜〜〜〜〜

Lorelei had been wandering the city. She hadn't known what to do after the captain's passing. The burden of the congregation seemed to choke her mind. She had managed to catch the captain's body before he fell, but he was gone. The eyes of the church... her church gazed up, searching for direction. She had barely been able to stumble over an excuse before fleeing. The sun had been in her eyes as she cried silently through the streets of the drowned city.

She walked down a shady promenade, stepping out into the

light in the square with open water in the middle. The sun felt good on her tired body and she tilted her head up to feel it. The light pricked at her puffy eyelids.

A scream struck Lorelei out of her trance. She started, opening her eyes to see a small figure hit the water hard. There was a woman on a lower bridge pointing and shouting at the place the figure had fallen.

She kicked off her old boots and dove for the cold, dark water.

~~~~~~~~~

"They killed my baby! They killed her and want to give me shut-up money! They won't even give me her body! I want you buzzards out of my house! I want you gone!" Tala wailed to the crowd outside their small home. The neighbors had gathered when they saw black suits waiting outside the mourning mother's home. Black suits meant trouble or money most times, both of which were the best kind of gossip. The girl's father was crushed by the news. Her mother was enraged. She'd lost one daughter to the rot and a son to the cults. The girl was her last child. Her grief echoed through the lower deck and caught flame. The black suits shuffled awkwardly away back to their roost.

The young people began to organize and speechify. The elders hung black banners and sang old songs of rebellion. The bridges to the upper decks were torn down by crowds of angry hands.

~~~~~~~~~

An emergency crew pushed their way through the crowd. There were onlookers from upper levels, but the crowd that gathered on the walkway surrounding where she fell was thick. There were the voyeurs who always showed up with tragedy and the concerned citizens and wide-eyed children. The dive crew was met with a young

woman kneeling on the boardwalk, her blue dress soaked and cling-
ing to her body, her wide eyes darted franticly, and her chest heaving.
She was clutching the small girl in her arms; blood from the girl's
temple was staining the fabric at her breast. The crew took the girl;
the woman resisted for a moment, then released her burden.

"I taste it, Captain. I taste it." she had been whispering to herself. Most likely shock, the emergency team reported. After the girl
had been taken Lorelei looked at the responder who had the girl.

"She's important. Be careful with her."

The girl was already dead.

~~~~~~~~

There were a few still nights after she fell. The lower decks
were grieving. The lantern boats they lit on the calm night water
made their memorial vigil a haunting view to the upper decks. The
well-to-do had a hard time sleeping because of the tension in the air.
The light coming from below bounced up the slick granite walls and
created an undying sunset they couldn't avoid, except to pull all the
curtains closed and be in unnatural darkness. They were left to listen
to the hymns and ululations that echoed to their nests. The noise was
worse in the dark. Fish weren't supposed to sing.

~~~~~~~~

The water was cold and deep and darker than it seemed it
should have been. Lorelei could see the small figure of the girl just
feet below her. She strained to swim faster while her breath began to
feel small and hard in her throat. The girl was sinking too fast.

But then she stopped sinking.

She was suspended in the water, almost as if a thread had been pulled from her narrow chest reaching up from the depths toward the surface. Lorelei started, a burst of bubbles coming from her mouth. She tried to swim farther to grab her but was also suspended, unable to move. The water began to warm and swirl around the pair. The pressure from Lorelei's lungs began to ease and she felt an impossible new breath in her chest. The girl began to glow, a soft blue-green light emanated from her chest. She opened her eyes, now glowing the same blue-green light, and spoke something incomprehensible to the woman in the water. Lorelei could only stare transfixed.

The warm current swirled and intertwined around the couple, cradling them. The light seemed to sooth and they drifted up and up toward the surface. Lorelei could almost hear singing in the water like a voice she knew once, but faint and far away. It felt like being home.

Then the light disappeared and the sea went cold and her lungs were burning and the girl was drifting once more. Lorelei grabbed the girl and pushed for the surface.

<div align="center">~~~~~~</div>

Nehiti Crane leaned on the railing of his penthouse balcony looking at the destruction below. He had a glass of wine swirling in his palm and a serious look on his face. Dr. Reiksac and Barron Holiday stared coolly across the space at each other. They'd been asked to have an audience with Crane, the most imposing man in the city. A wailing scream echoed over the distant noise, and Crane took a sip of a vintage. It was a bottle from before the city drowned, the taste was different somehow, less salty. He ran a dark hand over his shaven head.

"Mr. Crane, sir?" Holiday's voice was thinner than normal with a thread of fear weaving through it.

"A fine mess you two have made of my city," His voice was deep and had almost a sing-song cadence, "I do not blame you though." Holiday opened his mouth to speak, but Nehiti continued, "This was in the works far before the girl. A city needs to purge every so often. They will fight themselves out, and the chum will wash out to sea. A great catharsis of man. And we are lucky enough to have our safe perch up here, to witness the event."

He paused looking over the vista. There were fires, bridges burned and gasoline fires floating on the high tides. Riot police were cruising in boats and sectioning off different waterways. Neighborhoods had been sprayed with riot gas. Skin rot injections had already been embargoed. Twenty five people had succumbed in the last four days.

"Isn't it extraordinary, the nature of man?"